Ruth

An Illustrated Hebrew Reader's Edition

Adam J. Howell

Illustrated by Harvey E. Howell

Published by GlossaHouse, LLC

GlossaHouse, LLC
110 Callis Circle
Wilmore, KY 40390

Publisher's Cataloging-in-Publication Data

61 pages ; 25.4cm — (HA'ARETS)

ISBN: 978-1-63663-002-1

Library of Congress Control Number:

Printing in the United States of America

First printing, 2020

The Hebrew text in this book is from the Westminster Leningrad Codex found at https://tanach.us. The text follows the qere readings at https://tanach.us.

www.glossahouse.com

Made in the USA
Columbia, SC
06 February 2021

Ruth

An Illustrated Hebrew Reader's Edition

Adam J. Howell

Illustrated by Harvey E. Howell

HA'ARETS

HEBREW & ARAMAIC ACCESSIBLE RESOURCES
FOR EXEGETICAL AND THEOLOGICAL STUDIES

SERIES EDITORS

TRAVIS WEST   JESSE R. SCHEUMANN

GlossaHouse
Wilmore, KY
www.glossahouse.com

HA'ARETS

The Hebrew word הָאָרֶץ means "the earth, the land." It refers to the entirety of the physical world we see and touch and live upon. It is the creation of God, a gift for sustaining life and gladdening the heart, and it is the primary space of God's self-revelation. The HA'ARETS series—Hebrew & Aramaic Accessible Resources for Exegetical and Theological Studies—is an innovative curriculum suite offering resources that participate in the life-giving richness of הָאָרֶץ. The suite offers affordable and innovative print and electronic resources including grammars, readers, specialized studies, and other exegetical materials that encourage and foster the exegetical use of biblical Hebrew and Aramaic for the world and the global church.

Preface

The goal of this book is to provide an illustrated version of the Hebrew text of Ruth so that students may be able to associate images with the Hebrew text they are reading. As with any learning process, when the brain engages more neurons, students are more likely to retain the information they are learning. Here, we hope that you will be able to "enter into" the story of Ruth by means of these illustrations and not only retain new vocabulary because of an associated image, but also that you may be able to better understand grammatical constructions as they are interpreted visually.

We chose the book of Ruth primarily because of its placement in pedagogical sequences in Hebrew courses. Many Hebrew professors ask students to translate Ruth after a year of introductory Hebrew, and so for their students, Ruth is one of the first biblical books they read in the original language.

While attempting to create a resource that is useful for early Hebrew students, this book provides reader's footnotes wherein non-verbs occurring fewer than 100 times are glossed and verbs with roots occurring fewer than 100 times are glossed. The footnoted glosses are intended to be a contextually appropriate gloss. Reference works such as HALOT, BDB, DCH, and NIDOTTE were used to derive the glosses. For verbs, we have listed the tri-consonantal root letters. We hope this will be especially helpful for weak verbs in which original root letters are often missing. There is no further morphological discussion of weak verbs in this book, but hopefully the presence of the original root letters along with an abbreviation of the verbal stem in the footnotes will guide students to the morphological discussions in their first-year Hebrew textbooks for how various weaknesses affect verbal morphology. In addition to the footnoted glosses, this book includes a full glossary in the back with all vocabulary glosses in Ruth.

The Hebrew text in this book is from the Westminster Leningrad Codex found at https://tanach.us. The text follows the *qere* readings at https://tanach.us. Students should refer to a critical edition of the Hebrew Bible to get full information on each *ketiv/qere*. They are not marked in any special way in this book. An additional note should be made regarding the presence of a "dageshed *alef*" in a couple of places (e.g., Ruth 2:10, 11). This dagesh (mappiq?) does indeed occur in the Leningrad Codex, but it has been removed from the modern *Biblical Hebraica Stuttgartensia* (BHS) since the dagesh is absent in the Aleppo Codex. However, the newest edition of Biblica Hebraica, *Biblia Hebraica Quinta* (BHQ), adds these dageshim back into the text with critical notes pointing the reader to the appropriate manuscripts. I would imagine that with the addition of these dageshim into BHQ, they will become an item of discussion.

Throughout the book, you will see squared, grey text boxes for narrative text and rounded, white text boxes for direct speech. These are subtle, but intentional practices so that students can delineate clearly the speech type they are reading. Where speech is embedded two or three layers within the discourse, there are text boxes within text boxes. These will be apparent when encountered and will hopefully add to the visual value of the book. In order to follow the flow of this book, one should generally move from top to bottom on each page and from right to left.

As with any artistic rendering, sometimes explanation is needed. For this reason, we have provided an "Explanation of Select Images" before the glossary in order to explain some of the subtle details of the illustrations that would prove helpful for understanding the overall message of the book.

This book has been a labor of joy alongside my dad, Harvey E. Howell, as the artist for this work. Harvey meticulously read the book of Ruth many times and sought to situate himself in the worlds of Moab and Bethlehem during the period of the judges. To some degree, Dad became a character in the story, seeing the other characters live out this narrative as the scenes developed from the end of his pencil. This project would not be what it is without the artistic interpretations of a man who loves the Lord with all his heart, soul, and "veryness" (Deut 6:5).

We are grateful for the meticulous and helpful feedback from the editors of this series at GlossaHouse, Jesse Scheumann and Travis West. Through many emails and hundreds of Google Drive notifications, Jesse and Travis provided detailed notes and interpretive questions, all of which made this book a more helpful resource. I am greatly indebted to these men for their work and encouragement along the way.

Lastly, I want to thank my wife and family for giving me the space to work on projects like this. Liz, Noah, Tovah, Judah, and Norah, you all make this labor of joy exceedingly more joyful. You are gifts from the Lord to me and I'm thankful that we get to tackle these projects together.

—Adam J. Howell

Ruth

An Illustrated Hebrew Reader's Edition

פֶּרֶק
א

וַיְהִי בִּימֵי שְׁפֹט הַשֹּׁפְטִים
וַיְהִי רָעָב בָּאָרֶץ

וַיֵּלֶךְ אִישׁ מִבֵּית לֶחֶם יְהוּדָה לָגוּר[1] בִּשְׂדֵי מוֹאָב
הוּא וְאִשְׁתּוֹ וּשְׁנֵי בָנָיו:

[1] גוּר Q: to sojourn

וְשֵׁם הָאִישׁ אֱלִימֶ֫לֶךְ וְשֵׁם אִשְׁתּוֹ נָעֳמִי

וְשֵׁם שְׁנֵי־בָנָ֫יו ׀ מַחְלוֹן וְכִלְיוֹן אֶפְרָתִ֫ים מִבֵּית לֶ֫חֶם יְהוּדָֽה

וַיָּבֹ֫אוּ שְׂדֵי־מוֹאָב וַיִּֽהְיוּ־שָֽׁם׃

וַיָּ֤מָת אֱלִימֶ֙לֶךְ֙ אִ֣ישׁ נָעֳמִ֔י וַתִּשָּׁאֵ֥ר הִ֖יא וּשְׁנֵ֥י בָנֶֽיהָ׃

וַיִּשְׂא֣וּ לָהֶ֗ם נָשִׁים֙ מֹֽאֲבִיּ֔וֹת

שֵׁ֤ם הָֽאַחַת֙ עָרְפָּ֔ה

וְשֵׁ֥ם הַשֵּׁנִ֖ית ר֑וּת

וַיֵּ֥שְׁבוּ שָׁ֖ם כְּעֶ֥שֶׂר[1] שָׁנִֽים׃

1:3–4

[1] עֶ֥שֶׂר ten

וַיָּמֻ֥תוּ גַם־שְׁנֵיהֶ֖ם מַחְל֣וֹן וְכִלְי֑וֹן וַתִּשָּׁאֵר֙ הָֽאִשָּׁ֔ה מִשְּׁנֵ֥י יְלָדֶ֖יהָ[1] וּמֵאִישָֽׁהּ׃

וַתָּ֤קָם הִיא֙ וְכַלֹּתֶ֔יהָ[2] וַתָּ֖שָׁב מִשְּׂדֵ֥י מוֹאָ֑ב

כִּ֤י שָֽׁמְעָה֙ בִּשְׂדֵ֣ה מוֹאָ֔ב כִּֽי־פָקַ֤ד יְהוָה֙ אֶת־עַמּ֔וֹ לָתֵ֥ת לָהֶ֖ם לָֽחֶם׃

וַתֵּצֵ֗א מִן־הַמָּקוֹם֙ אֲשֶׁ֣ר הָֽיְתָה־שָׁ֔מָּה וּשְׁתֵּ֥י כַלֹּתֶ֖יהָ[2] עִמָּ֑הּ וַתֵּלַ֣כְנָה בַדֶּ֔רֶךְ לָשׁ֖וּב אֶל־אֶ֥רֶץ יְהוּדָֽה׃

1:5–7

[1] יֶ֫לֶד male child   [2] כַּלָּה daughter-in-law

וַתֹּאמֶר נָעֳמִי לִשְׁתֵּי כַלֹּתֶיהָ[1]

לֵכְנָה שֹּׁבְנָה אִשָּׁה לְבֵית אִמָּהּ
יַעַשׂ יְהוָה עִמָּכֶם חֶסֶד
כַּאֲשֶׁר עֲשִׂיתֶם עִם־הַמֵּתִים וְעִמָּדִי[2]:
יִתֵּן יְהוָה לָכֶם וּמְצֶאןָ מְנוּחָה[3]
אִשָּׁה בֵּית אִישָׁהּ

וַתִּשַּׁק[4] לָהֶן וַתִּשֶּׂאנָה קוֹלָן וַתִּבְכֶּינָה:

1:8–9

[1] כַּלָּה daughter-in-law [2] עִמָּד long form of עִם, "with" [3] מְנוּחָה rest [4] נשׁק Q: to kiss

וַתֹּאמַרְנָה־לָּ֑הּ

כִּי־אִתָּ֥ךְ נָשׁ֖וּב לְעַמֵּֽךְ׃

וַתֹּ֣אמֶר נׇעֳמִ֗י

שֹׁ֤בְנָה בְנֹתַי֙ לָ֣מָּה תֵלַ֣כְנָה עִמִּ֔י
הַֽעֽוֹד־לִ֤י בָנִים֙ בְּמֵעַ֔י [1]
וְהָי֥וּ לָכֶ֖ם לַאֲנָשִֽׁים׃
שֹׁ֤בְנָה בְנֹתַי֙ לֵ֔כְןָ
כִּ֥י זָקַ֖נְתִּי [2] מִהְי֣וֹת לְאִ֑ישׁ
כִּ֤י אָמַ֨רְתִּי֙ יֶשׁ־לִ֣י תִקְוָ֔ה [3]
גַּ֣ם הָיִ֤יתִי הַלַּ֨יְלָה֙ לְאִ֔ישׁ
וְגַ֖ם יָלַ֥דְתִּי בָנִֽים׃
הֲלָהֵ֣ן ׀ תְּשַׂבֵּ֗רְנָה [5] עַ֚ד אֲשֶׁ֣ר יִגְדָּ֔לוּ
הֲלָהֵן֙ תֵּֽעָגֵ֔נָה [6] לְבִלְתִּ֖י הֱי֣וֹת לְאִ֑ישׁ
אַ֣ל בְּנֹתַ֗י כִּי־מַר־לִ֤י מְאֹד֙ מִכֶּ֔ם [7]
כִּֽי־יָצְאָ֥ה בִ֖י יַד־יְהֹוָֽה׃

1:10–13

---

^{1} מֵעָה womb ^{2} זקן Q: to be old ^{3} תִּקְוָה hope ^{4} לָהֵן therefore ^{5} שָׂבַר PI: to wait for ^{6} עגן NI: to be hindered ^{7} מרר Q: to be bitter

וַתִּשֶּׂנָה קוֹלָן וַתִּבְכֶּינָה עֽוֹד

וַתִּשַּׁק¹ עָרְפָּה֙ לַחֲמוֹתָ֔הּ²

וְר֖וּת דָּ֥בְקָה³ בָּֽהּ׃

1:14

¹ נשק Q: to kiss ² חָמוֹת mother-in-law ³ דבק Q: to cling

וַתֹּ֗אמֶר

הִנֵּה֙ שָׁ֣בָה יְבִמְתֵּ֔ךְ אֶל־עַמָּ֖הּ וְאֶל־אֱלֹהֶ֑יהָ¹
שׁ֖וּבִי אַחֲרֵ֥י יְבִמְתֵּֽךְ¹:

וַתֹּ֣אמֶר רוּת֩

אַל־תִּפְגְּעִי־בִ֔י²לְעָזְבֵ֖ךְ לָשׁ֥וּב מֵאַחֲרָ֑יִךְ
כִּ֠י אֶל־אֲשֶׁ֨ר תֵּלְכִ֜י אֵלֵ֗ךְ
וּבַאֲשֶׁ֤ר תָּלִ֙ינִי֙³ אָלִ֔ין
עַמֵּ֣ךְ עַמִּ֔י וֵאלֹהַ֖יִךְ אֱלֹהָֽי:
בַּאֲשֶׁ֤ר תָּמ֙וּתִי֙ אָמ֔וּת וְשָׁ֖ם אֶקָּבֵ֑ר
כֹּה֩ יַעֲשֶׂ֨ה יְהוָ֥ה לִ֛י וְכֹ֥ה יֹסִ֖יף
כִּ֣י הַמָּ֔וֶת יַפְרִ֥יד⁴ בֵּינִ֖י וּבֵינֵֽךְ:

וַתֵּ֕רֶא כִּֽי־מִתְאַמֶּ֥צֶת⁵ הִ֖יא
לָלֶ֣כֶת אִתָּ֑הּ
וַתֶּחְדַּ֖ל⁶ לְדַבֵּ֥ר אֵלֶֽיהָ:

¹יְבָמָה brother's widow ²פגע Q: to urge ³לין Q: to lodge ⁴פרד HI: to separate ⁵אמץ HTP: to be strong ⁶חדל Q: to cease

וַתֵּלַ֣כְנָה שְׁתֵּיהֶ֔ם עַד־בֹּאָ֖נָה בֵּ֣ית לָ֑חֶם

וַיְהִ֗י כְּבֹאָ֙נָה֙ בֵּ֣ית לֶ֔חֶם וַתֵּהֹ֤ם¹ כָּל־הָעִיר֙ עֲלֵיהֶ֔ן

וַתֹּאמַ֖רְנָה

הֲזֹ֥את נָעֳמִֽי׃

¹הום NI: to be in a stir, to "hum"

וַתֹּאמֶר אֲלֵיהֶן

אַל־תִּקְרֶאנָה לִי נָעֳמִי קְרֶאןָ לִי מָרָא
כִּי־הֵמַר¹ שַׁדַּי² לִי מְאֹד: אֲנִי מְלֵאָה³ הָלַכְתִּי
וְרֵיקָם⁴ הֱשִׁיבַנִי יְהוָה לָמָּה תִקְרֶאנָה לִי נָעֳמִי
וַיהוָה עָנָה בִי וְשַׁדַּי² הֵרַע⁵ לִי:

וַתָּשָׁב נָעֳמִי וְר֫וּת הַמּוֹאֲבִיָּה כַלָּתָהּ⁶ עִמָּהּ
הַשָּׁבָה מִשְּׂדֵי מוֹאָב
וְהֵמָּה בָּאוּ בֵּית לֶחֶם
בִּתְחִלַּת⁷ קְצִיר⁸ שְׂעֹרִים⁹:

1:20–22

¹מרר HI: to make bitter   ²שַׁדַּי Almighty   ³מָלֵא full   ⁴רֵיקָם in an empty condition   ⁵רעע HI: to do calamity
⁶כַּלָּה daughter-in-law   ⁷תְּחִלָּה beginning   ⁸קָצִיר harvest   ⁹שְׂעֹרָה barley

פרק ב

וּלְנָעֳמִי מוֹדָע[1] לְאִישָׁהּ
אִישׁ גִּבּוֹר חַיִל
מִמִּשְׁפַּחַת אֱלִימֶלֶךְ

וּשְׁמוֹ בֹּעַז:

2:1

[1] מוֹדָע relative

וַתֹּאמֶר֩ ר֨וּת הַמּוֹאֲבִיָּ֜ה אֶֽל־נָעֳמִ֗י

אֵלְכָה־נָּ֤א הַשָּׂדֶה֙ וַאֲלַקֳטָ֣ה בַשִּׁבֳּלִ֔ים[2] אַחַ֕ר אֲשֶׁ֥ר אֶמְצָא־חֵ֖ן[3] בְּעֵינָ֑יו

וַתֹּ֥אמֶר לָ֖הּ

לְכִ֥י בִתִּֽי:

וַתֵּ֤לֶךְ וַתָּבוֹא֙ וַתְּלַקֵּט֙[1] בַּשָּׂדֶ֔ה אַחֲרֵ֖י הַקֹּצְרִ֑ים[4]

וַיִּ֣קֶר[5] מִקְרֶ֔הָ[6] חֶלְקַ֥ת[7] הַשָּׂדֶ֖ה לְבֹ֑עַז אֲשֶׁ֖ר מִמִּשְׁפַּ֥חַת אֱלִימֶֽלֶךְ:

2:2–3

[1] לקט PI: to glean [2] שִׁבֹּלֶת ear of grain [3] חֵן favor [4] קצר Q: to reap [5] קרה Q: to happen to (coincidence) [6] מִקְרֶה incident, chance [7] חֶלְקָה portion

וְהִנֵּה־בֹעַז בָּא מִבֵּית לֶחֶם

וַיֹּאמֶר לַקּוֹצְרִים¹

יְהוָה עִמָּכֶם

וַיֹּאמְרוּ לוֹ

יְבָרֶכְךָ יְהוָה:

וַיֹּאמֶר בֹּעַז לְנַעֲרוֹ הַנִּצָּב² עַל־הַקּוֹצְרִים¹

לְמִי הַנַּעֲרָה³ הַזֹּאת:

2:4–5

¹ קצר Q: to reap   ² נצב NI: to stand, be stationed   ³ נַעֲרָה young woman

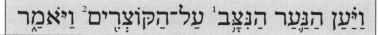

וַיַּעַן הַנַּעַר הַנִּצָּב¹ עַל־הַקּוֹצְרִים² וַיֹּאמַר

נַעֲרָה³ מוֹאֲבִיָּה הִיא הַשָּׁבָה עִם־נָעֳמִי מִשְּׂדֵה מוֹאָב:

וַתֹּאמֶר

אֲלַקֳטָה⁴־נָּא וְאָסַפְתִּי בָעֳמָרִים⁵ אַחֲרֵי הַקּוֹצְרִים²

וַתָּבוֹא וַתַּעֲמוֹד מֵאָז הַבֹּקֶר וְעַד־עַתָּה זֶה שִׁבְתָּהּ הַבַּיִת מְעָט:

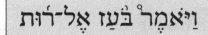

וַיֹּאמֶר בֹּעַז אֶל־רוּת

הֲלוֹא שָׁמַעַתְּ בִּתִּי אַל־תֵּלְכִי לִלְקֹט⁶ בְּשָׂדֶה אַחֵר וְגַם לֹא תַעֲבוּרִי מִזֶּה וְכֹה תִדְבָּקִין⁷ עִם־נַעֲרֹתָי³:

2:6–8

¹נצב NI: to stand, be stationed ²קצר Q: to reap ³נַעֲרָה young woman ⁴לקט PI: to glean ⁵עֹמֶר sheaf
⁶לקט Q: to glean ⁷דבק Q: to cling

2:9–10

¹קצר Q: to reap ²צמא Q: to be thirsty ³שאב Q: to draw (water) ⁴מַדּוּעַ why? ⁵חֵן favor ⁶נכר HI: to recognize ⁷נָכְרִיָּה (female) foreigner

הֻגֵּד הֻגַּד לִי כֹּל אֲשֶׁר־עָשִׂית אֶת־חֲמוֹתֵךְ¹ אַחֲרֵי מוֹת אִישֵׁךְ

וַתַּעַזְבִי אָבִיךְ וְאִמֵּךְ וְאֶרֶץ מוֹלַדְתֵּךְ²

וַתֵּלְכִי אֶל־עַם אֲשֶׁר לֹא־יָדַעַתְּ תְּמוֹל שִׁלְשׁוֹם³:

יְשַׁלֵּם יְהוָה פׇּעֳלֵךְ⁴ וּתְהִי מַשְׂכֻּרְתֵּךְ⁵ שְׁלֵמָה⁶ מֵעִם יְהוָה אֱלֹהֵי יִשְׂרָאֵל

אֲשֶׁר־בָּאת לַחֲסוֹת⁷ תַּחַת־כְּנָפָיו:

אֶמְצָא־חֵן⁸ בְּעֵינֶיךָ אֲדֹנִי כִּי נִחַמְתָּנִי

וְכִי דִבַּרְתָּ עַל־לֵב שִׁפְחָתֶךָ⁹

וְאָנֹכִי לֹא אֶהְיֶה כְּאַחַת שִׁפְחֹתֶיךָ⁹:

2:11–13

¹חֲמוֹת mother-in-law ²מוֹלֶדֶת kindred ³תְּמוֹל שִׁלְשׁוֹם previously (lit. day before yesterday) ⁴פֹּעַל work ⁵מַשְׂכֹּרֶת wages
⁶שָׁלֵם complete, full ⁷חסה Q: to seek refuge ⁸חֵן favor ⁹שִׁפְחָה maid-servant

וַיֹּאמֶר לָהּ בֹּעַז לְעֵת הָאֹכֶל[1]

גֹּשִׁי הֲלֹם[2] וְאָכַלְתְּ מִן־הַלֶּחֶם
וְטָבַלְתְּ[3] פִּתֵּךְ[4] בַּחֹמֶץ[5]

וַתֵּשֶׁב מִצַּד[6] הַקּוֹצְרִים[7] וַיִּצְבָּט[8]־לָהּ קָלִי[9]
וַתֹּאכַל וַתִּשְׂבַּע[10] וַתֹּתַר:

2:14

[1] אֹכֶל food [2] הֲלֹם here [3] טבל Q: to dip [4] פַּת morsel [5] חֹמֶץ vinegar [6] צַד side [7] קצר Q: to reap [8] צבט Q: to hold out
[9] קָלִי parched/roasted grain [10] שבע Q: to be satisfied

וַתָּ֙קָם֙ לְלַקֵּ֔ט¹

וַיְצַ֙ו בֹּ֜עַז אֶת־נְעָרָ֤יו לֵאמֹ֔ר

גַּ֣ם בֵּ֧ין הָעֳמָרִ֛ים² תְּלַקֵּ֖ט
וְלֹ֥א תַכְלִימֽוּהָ³ :
וְגַ֛ם שֹׁל־תָּשֹׁ֥לּוּ⁴ לָ֖הּ מִן־הַצְּבָתִ֑ים⁵
וַעֲזַבְתֶּ֥ם וְלִקְּטָ֖ה וְלֹ֥א תִגְעֲרוּ⁷־בָֽהּ⁶ :

2:15–16

¹לקט PI: to glean ²עֹמֶר sheaf ³כלם HI: to humiliate ⁴שׁלל Q: to pull out ⁵צֶבֶת bundle ⁶גער Q: to rebuke

וַתְּלַקֵּט֤ בַּשָּׂדֶה֙ עַד־הָעָ֔רֶב
וַתַּחְבֹּט֙ אֵ֣ת אֲשֶׁר־לִקֵּ֔טָה
וַיְהִ֖י כְּאֵיפָ֥ה שְׂעֹרִֽים׃

וַתִּשָּׂא֙ וַתָּב֣וֹא הָעִ֔יר
וַתֵּ֥רֶא חֲמוֹתָ֖הּ אֵ֣ת אֲשֶׁר־לִקֵּ֑טָה
וַתּוֹצֵא֙ וַתִּתֶּן־לָ֔הּ
אֵ֥ת אֲשֶׁר־הוֹתִ֖רָה מִשָּׂבְעָֽהּ׃

2:17–18

¹ לקט PI: to glean ² חבט Q: to beat out ³ אֵיפָה a grain measure = 20 dry quarts ⁴ שְׂעֹרָה barley ⁵ חֲמוֹת mother-in-law ⁶ שֹׂבַע satisfaction, abundance

וַתֹּאמֶר לָהּ חֲמוֹתָהּ[1]

אֵיפֹה[2] לִקַּטְתְּ[3] הַיּוֹם
וְאָנָה[4] עָשִׂית
יְהִי מַכִּירֵךְ[5] בָּרוּךְ

וַתַּגֵּד לַחֲמוֹתָהּ[1]
אֵת אֲשֶׁר־עָשְׂתָה עִמּוֹ
וַתֹּאמֶר

שֵׁם הָאִישׁ אֲשֶׁר עָשִׂיתִי עִמּוֹ הַיּוֹם בֹּעַז:

וַתֹּאמֶר נָעֳמִי לְכַלָּתָהּ[6]
בָּרוּךְ הוּא לַיהוָה
אֲשֶׁר לֹא־עָזַב חַסְדּוֹ
אֶת־הַחַיִּים וְאֶת־הַמֵּתִים

2:19–20a

[1]חָמוֹת mother-in-law [2]אֵיפֹה where? [3]לקט PI: to glean [4]אָן where? [5]נכר HI: to recognize [6]כַּלָּה daughter-in-law

וַתֹּאמֶר לָהּ נָעֳמִי

קָרוֹב¹ לָנוּ הָאִישׁ
מִגֹּאֲלֵנוּ הוּא:

וַתֹּאמֶר רוּת הַמּוֹאֲבִיָּה

גַּם | כִּי־אָמַר אֵלַי
עִם־הַנְּעָרִים אֲשֶׁר־לִי תִּדְבָּקִין²
עַד אִם־כִּלּוּ אֵת כָּל־הַקָּצִיר³ אֲשֶׁר־לִי:

וַתֹּאמֶר נָעֳמִי אֶל־רוּת כַּלָּתָהּ⁴

טוֹב בִּתִּי כִּי תֵצְאִי עִם־נַעֲרוֹתָיו⁵
וְלֹא יִפְגְּעוּ־בָךְ⁶ בְּשָׂדֶה אַחֵר:

2:20b–22

¹קָרוֹב near (relative)   ²דבק Q: to cling   ³קָצִיר harvest   ⁴כַּלָּה daughter-in-law   ⁵נַעֲרָה young woman   ⁶פגע Q: to assault

וַתִּדְבַּ֞ק בְּנַעֲר֥וֹת² בֹּ֖עַז לְלַקֵּ֑ט³
עַד־כְּל֥וֹת קְצִֽיר־הַשְּׂעֹרִים֙⁴ וּקְצִ֣יר הַֽחִטִּ֔ים⁵
וַתֵּ֖שֶׁב אֶת־חֲמוֹתָֽהּ׃⁶

¹דבק Q: to cling ²נַעֲרָה young woman ³לקט PI: to glean ⁴קְצִיר־שְׂעֹרִים barley harvest ⁵קְצִיר־חִטִּים wheat harvest
⁶חָמוֹת mother-in-law

פֶּרֶק ג

וַתֹּאמֶר לָהּ נָעֳמִי חֲמוֹתָהּ[1]

בִּתִּי הֲלֹא אֲבַקֶּשׁ־לָךְ מָנוֹחַ[2] אֲשֶׁר יִיטַב־לָךְ:
וְעַתָּה הֲלֹא בֹעַז מֹדַעְתָּנוּ[3] אֲשֶׁר הָיִית אֶת־נַעֲרוֹתָיו[4]

הִנֵּה־הוּא זֹרֶה[5] אֶת־גֹּרֶן[6] הַשְּׂעֹרִים[7] הַלָּיְלָה:
וְרָחַצְתְּ[8] ׀ וָסַכְתְּ[9] וְשַׂמְתְּ שִׂמְלֹתַיִךְ[10] עָלַיִךְ וְיָרַדְתְּ הַגֹּרֶן[6]
אַל־תִּוָּדְעִי לָאִישׁ עַד כַּלֹּתוֹ לֶאֱכֹל וְלִשְׁתּוֹת:

3:1–3

[1] חָמוֹת mother-in-law [2] מָנוֹחַ rest [3] מֹדַעַת kindred [4] נַעֲרָה young woman [5] זרה Q: to winnow [6] גֹּרֶן threshing floor [7] שְׂעֹרָה barley [8] רחץ Q: to wash [9] סוך Q: to anoint [10] שִׂמְלָה cloak, mantle

וַיְהִי בְשָׁכְבוֹ וְיָדַעַתְּ אֶת־הַמָּקוֹם אֲשֶׁר יִשְׁכַּב־שָׁם

וּבָאת וְגִלִּית מַרְגְּלֹתָיו[1] וְשָׁכָבְתְּ

3:4a

[1] מַרְגְּלֹת place of the feet

וְהוּא יַגִּיד לָךְ אֵת אֲשֶׁר תַּעֲשִׂין:

3:4b

וַתֹּאמֶר אֵלֶיהָ

כֹּל אֲשֶׁר־תֹּאמְרִי אֵלַי אֶעֱשֶׂה:

וַתֵּרֶד הַגֹּרֶן[1] וַתַּעַשׂ כְּכֹל אֲשֶׁר־צִוַּתָּה חֲמוֹתָהּ[2]:

[1] גֹּרֶן threshing floor [2] חָמוֹת mother-in-law

וַיֹּ֨אכַל בֹּ֤עַז וַיֵּשְׁתְּ֙ וַיִּיטַ֣ב לִבּ֔וֹ
וַיָּבֹ֕א לִשְׁכַּ֖ב בִּקְצֵ֣ה הָעֲרֵמָ֑ה

וַתָּבֹ֣א בַלָּ֔ט וַתְּגַ֥ל מַרְגְּלֹתָ֖יו וַתִּשְׁכָּֽב׃

3:7

¹ קָצֶה end, extremity ² עֲרֵמָה heap ³ לָט secrecy ⁴ מַרְגְּלוֹת place of the feet

וַיְהִי֙ בַּחֲצִ֣י הַלַּ֔יְלָה וַיֶּחֱרַ֥ד הָאִ֖ישׁ וַיִּלָּפֵ֑ת[1] [2] וְהִנֵּ֣ה אִשָּׁ֔ה שֹׁכֶ֖בֶת מַרְגְּלֹתָֽיו[3]:

וַיֹּ֖אמֶר

מִי־אָ֑תְּ[4]

וַתֹּ֗אמֶר

אָנֹכִי֙ ר֣וּת אֲמָתֶ֔ךָ[5] וּפָרַשְׂתָּ֤[6] כְנָפֶ֙ךָ֙ עַל־אֲמָ֣תְךָ֔[5] כִּ֥י גֹאֵ֖ל אָֽתָּה׃

[1]חרד Q: to be startled [2]לפת NI: to turn (with grasping) [3]מַרְגְּלוֹת place of the feet [4]אַתְּ you (2fs) [5]אָמָה maidservant
[6]פרשׂ Q: to spread

וַיֹּאמֶר

בְּרוּכָה אַתְּ¹ לַיהוָה בִּתִּי הֵיטַבְתְּ חַסְדֵּךְ הָאַחֲרוֹן² מִן־הָרִאשׁוֹן
לְבִלְתִּי־לֶכֶת אַחֲרֵי הַבַּחוּרִים³ אִם־דַּל⁴ וְאִם־עָשִׁיר⁵:
וְעַתָּה בִּתִּי אַל־תִּירְאִי כֹּל אֲשֶׁר־תֹּאמְרִי אֶעֱשֶׂה־לָּךְ
כִּי יוֹדֵעַ כָּל־שַׁעַר עַמִּי כִּי אֵשֶׁת חַיִל אָתְּ¹:
וְעַתָּה כִּי אָמְנָם⁶ כִּי גֹאֵל אָנֹכִי

וְגַם יֵשׁ גֹּאֵל קָרוֹב⁷ מִמֶּנִּי:

לִינִי⁸ | הַלַּיְלָה וְהָיָה בַבֹּקֶר אִם־יִגְאָלֵךְ טוֹב יִגְאָל
וְאִם־לֹא יַחְפֹּץ⁹ לְגָאֳלֵךְ וּגְאַלְתִּיךְ אָנֹכִי חַי־יְהוָה
שִׁכְבִי עַד־הַבֹּקֶר:

וַתִּשְׁכַּב מַרְגְּלוֹתָיו¹⁰ עַד־הַבֹּקֶר

3:10–14a

¹ אַתְּ you (2fs) ² אַחֲרוֹן last ³ בָּחוּר (eligible) young man ⁴ דַּל poor ⁵ עָשִׁיר rich ⁶ אָמְנָם surely, indeed ⁷ קָרוֹב near
⁸ לִין Q: to lodge ⁹ חפץ Q: to delight ¹⁰ מַרְגְּלוֹת place of the feet

וַתָּ֫קָם בְּטֶ֫רֶם¹ יַכִּיר² אִישׁ אֶת־רֵעֵ֑הוּ

וַיֹּ֫אמֶר

אַל־יִוָּדַ֕ע כִּי־בָ֥אָה הָאִשָּׁ֖ה הַגֹּֽרֶן³׃

וַיֹּ֫אמֶר

הָ֫בִי⁴ הַמִּטְפַּ֫חַת⁵ אֲשֶׁר־עָלַ֫יִךְ וְאֶֽחֳזִי־בָ֑הּ⁶

וַתֹּ֫אחֶז⁶ בָּ֗הּ וַיָּ֫מָד⁷ שֵׁשׁ־שְׂעֹרִים⁸ וַיָּ֫שֶׁת⁹ עָלֶ֑יהָ

3:14b–15a

¹ טֶ֫רֶם before, not yet   ² נכר HI: to recognize   ³ גֹּ֫רֶן threshing floor   ⁴ יהב Q: to give   ⁵ מִטְפַּ֫חַת cloak   ⁶ אחז Q: to grasp
⁷ מדד Q: to measure   ⁸ שְׂעֹרָה barley   ⁹ שׁית Q: to put, place

וַיָּבֹא הָעִיר׃

וַתָּבוֹא אֶל־חֲמוֹתָהּ¹

וַתֹּאמֶר

מִי־אַתְּ² בִּתִּי

וַתַּגֶּד־לָהּ אֵת כָּל־אֲשֶׁר עָשָׂה־לָהּ הָאִישׁ׃

3:15b–16

¹חֲמוֹת mother-in-law ²אַתְּ you (2fs)

וַתֹּ֫אמֶר

שֵׁשׁ־הַשְּׂעֹרִ֧ים¹ הָאֵ֛לֶּה נָ֥תַן לִ֖י כִּ֥י אָמַ֣ר אֵלַ֔י
אַל־תָּב֥וֹאִי רֵיקָ֖ם² אֶל־חֲמוֹתֵֽךְ³:

וַתֹּ֫אמֶר֙

שְׁבִ֣י בִתִּ֔י עַ֚ד אֲשֶׁ֣ר תֵּֽדְעִ֔ין
אֵ֖יךְ⁴ יִפֹּ֣ל דָּבָ֑ר
כִּ֣י לֹ֤א יִשְׁקֹט֙⁵ הָאִ֔ישׁ
כִּֽי־אִם־כִּלָּ֥ה הַדָּבָ֖ר הַיּֽוֹם:

¹שְׂעֹרָה barley ²רֵיקָם in an empty condition ³חֲמוֹת mother-in-law ⁴אֵיךְ how ⁵שקט Q: to be quiet, to be at rest

פְּלֹנִי אַלְמֹנִי[1] "So-And-So" (lit. 'a certain someone')

וַיִּקַּח עֲשָׂרָה¹ אֲנָשִׁים מִזִּקְנֵי הָעִיר וַיֹּאמֶר

שְׁבוּ־פֹה

וַיֵּשֵׁבוּ:

וַיֹּאמֶר לַגֹּאֵל

חֶלְקַת² הַשָּׂדֶה אֲשֶׁר לְאָחִינוּ לֶאֱלִימֶלֶךְ
מָכְרָה³ נׇעֳמִי הַשָּׁבָה מִשְּׂדֵה מוֹאָב:
וַאֲנִי אָמַרְתִּי אֶגְלֶה אׇזְנְךָ לֵאמֹר
קְנֵה⁴ נֶגֶד הַיֹּשְׁבִים וְנֶגֶד זִקְנֵי עַמִּי
אִם־תִּגְאַל גְּאָל וְאִם־לֹא יִגְאַל
הַגִּידָה לִּי וְאֵדְעָה כִּי אֵין זוּלָתְךָ⁵ לִגְאוֹל
וְאָנֹכִי אַחֲרֶיךָ

וַיֹּאמֶר

אָנֹכִי אֶגְאָל:

4:2–4

¹ עֲשָׂרָה ten ² חֶלְקָה portion ³ מכר Q: to sell ⁴ קנה Q: to acquire ⁵ זוּלָה except

וַיֹּאמֶר בֹּעַז

בְּיוֹם־קְנוֹתְךָ֧ הַשָּׂדֶ֛ה מִיַּ֥ד נָעֳמִ֖י
וּ֠מֵאֵת ר֣וּת הַמּוֹאֲבִיָּ֞ה אֵֽשֶׁת־הַמֵּ֤ת קָנִ֙יתָ֙
לְהָקִ֥ים שֵׁם־הַמֵּ֖ת עַל־נַחֲלָתֽוֹ׃

וַיֹּאמֶר הַגֹּאֵל

לֹ֤א אוּכַל֙ לִגְאָל־לִ֔י
פֶּן־אַשְׁחִ֖ית אֶת־נַחֲלָתִ֑י
גְּאַל־לְךָ֤ אַתָּה֙ אֶת־גְּאֻלָּתִ֔י
כִּ֥י לֹא־אוּכַ֖ל לִגְאֹֽל׃

4:5–6

¹קנה Q: to acquire ²גְּאֻלָּה redemption right(s)

וְזֹאת לְפָנִים בְּיִשְׂרָאֵל עַל־הַגְּאוּלָּה¹ וְעַל־הַתְּמוּרָה² לְקַיֵּם כָּל־דָּבָר שָׁלַף³ אִישׁ נַעֲלוֹ⁴ וְנָתַן לְרֵעֵהוּ וְזֹאת הַתְּעוּדָה⁵ בְּיִשְׂרָאֵל:

וַיֹּאמֶר הַגֹּאֵל לְבֹעַז

קְנֵה־לָךְ⁶

וַיִּשְׁלֹף³ נַעֲלוֹ⁴:

וַיֹּאמֶר בֹּעַז לַזְּקֵנִים וְכָל־הָעָם

עֵדִים⁷ אַתֶּם הַיּוֹם כִּי קָנִיתִי⁶ אֶת־כָּל־אֲשֶׁר לֶאֱלִימֶלֶךְ וְאֵת כָּל־אֲשֶׁר לְכִלְיוֹן וּמַחְלוֹן מִיַּד נָעֳמִי: וְגַם אֶת־רוּת הַמֹּאֲבִיָּה אֵשֶׁת מַחְלוֹן קָנִיתִי⁶ לִי לְאִשָּׁה לְהָקִים שֵׁם־הַמֵּת עַל־נַחֲלָתוֹ וְלֹא־יִכָּרֵת שֵׁם־הַמֵּת מֵעִם אֶחָיו וּמִשַּׁעַר מְקוֹמוֹ עֵדִים⁷ אַתֶּם הַיּוֹם:

4:7–10

¹גְּאֻלָּה redemption right(s) ²תְּמוּרָה exchange ³שָׁלַף Q: to pull off ⁴נַעַל sandal ⁵תְּעוּדָה confirmation ⁶קָנָה Q: to acquire ⁷עֵד witness

וַיֹּאמְרוּ כָּל־הָעָם אֲשֶׁר־בַּשַּׁעַר וְהַזְּקֵנִים עֵדִים¹

4:11a

¹עֵד witness

יִתֵּן֩ יְהֹוָ֨ה אֶת־הָאִשָּׁ֜ה הַבָּאָ֣ה אֶל־בֵּיתֶ֗ךָ

וּכְלֵאָה֙

כְּרָחֵ֤ל ׀

אֲשֶׁ֨ר בָּנ֤וּ שְׁתֵּיהֶם֙ אֶת־בֵּ֣ית יִשְׂרָאֵ֔ל

וַעֲשֵׂה־חַ֣יִל בְּאֶפְרָ֔תָה וּקְרָא־שֵׁ֖ם בְּבֵ֥ית לָֽחֶם׃

וִיהִ֤י בֵֽיתְךָ֙ כְּבֵ֣ית פֶּ֔רֶץ אֲשֶׁר־יָלְדָ֥ה תָמָ֖ר לִֽיהוּדָ֑ה
מִן־הַזֶּ֗רַע אֲשֶׁ֨ר יִתֵּ֤ן יְהוָה֙ לְךָ֔ מִן־הַֽנַּעֲרָ֖ה[1] הַזֹּֽאת׃

[1] נַעֲרָה young woman

וַיִּקַּח בֹּעַז אֶת־רוּת וַתְּהִי־לֹו לְאִשָּׁה וַיָּבֹא אֵלֶיהָ

וַיִּתֵּן יְהוָה לָהּ הֵרָיֹון[1] וַתֵּלֶד בֵּן׃

4:13

[1] הֵרָיֹון conception

וַתֹּאמַרְנָה הַנָּשִׁים אֶל־נָעֳמִי

בָּרוּךְ יְהֹוָה
אֲשֶׁר לֹא הִשְׁבִּית¹ לָךְ גֹּאֵל הַיּוֹם
וְיִקָּרֵא שְׁמוֹ בְּיִשְׂרָאֵל:

וְהָיָה לָךְ לְמֵשִׁיב נֶפֶשׁ וּלְכַלְכֵּל² אֶת־שֵׂיבָתֵךְ³
כִּי כַלָּתֵךְ⁴ אֲשֶׁר־אֲהֵבָתֶךְ יְלָדַתּוּ
אֲשֶׁר־הִיא טוֹבָה לָךְ מִשִּׁבְעָה בָּנִים:

4:14–15

¹ שבת HI: to leave without ²כול PILPEL: to sustain ³שֵׂיבָה old age ⁴כַּלָּה daughter-in-law

וַתִּקַּ֨ח נָעֳמִ֤י אֶת־הַיֶּ֙לֶד֙¹ וַתְּשִׁתֵ֣הוּ² בְחֵיקָ֔ה³ וַתְּהִי־ל֖וֹ לְאֹמֶֽנֶת⁴:

וַתִּקְרֶ֩אנָה֩ ל֨וֹ הַשְּׁכֵנ֥וֹת⁵ שֵׁם֙ לֵאמֹ֔ר

יֻלַּד־בֵּ֖ן לְנָעֳמִ֑י

וַתִּקְרֶ֤אנָה שְׁמוֹ֙ עוֹבֵ֔ד

ה֥וּא אֲבִי־יִשַׁ֖י אֲבִ֥י דָוִֽד:

¹יֶ֫לֶד male child ²שִׁית Q: to place ³חֵיק lap, bosom ⁴אֹמֶ֫נֶת foster-nurse ⁵שְׁכֵנָה neighborhood woman

פֶּרֶץ הוֹלִיד אֶת־חֶצְרוֹן:
וְחֶצְרוֹן הוֹלִיד אֶת־רָם
וְרָם הוֹלִיד אֶת־עַמִּינָדָב:
וְעַמִּינָדָב הוֹלִיד אֶת־נַחְשׁוֹן
וְנַחְשׁוֹן הוֹלִיד אֶת־שַׂלְמָה:
וְשַׂלְמוֹן הוֹלִיד אֶת־בֹּעַז
וּבֹעַז הוֹלִיד אֶת־עוֹבֵד:
וְעֹבֵד הוֹלִיד אֶת־יִשָׁי
וְיִשַׁי הוֹלִיד אֶת־דָּוִד:

4:18–22

[1] תוֹלְדוֹת generations

Explanations of Select Images

<u>Ruth 2:1</u> – וּשְׁמ֖וֹ בֹּ֑עַז... "… and his name [was] Boaz." In this illustration, the final clause is intentionally separate from the rest of the text. The placement of the *athnaḥ* so late in this verse causes the reader to "wait" until the end of the verse to hear the name of this character who is a near relative and a "mighty man of valor." As the verse begins, the reader surely anticipates that this man will help Ruth and Naomi, and indeed this is his initial introduction in the book. However, the narrative that resumes after this image (Ruth 2:2ff) involves Naomi and Ruth conversing about gleaning in the fields. Boaz is here intentionally emphasized, and so the large illustration and placement of text in a separate box was a desire to highlight that emphasis.

<u>Ruth 2:2</u> – וַתֹּאמֶר֩ ר֨וּת הַמּוֹאֲבִיָּ֜ה אֶֽל־נָעֳמִ֗י... "…and Ruth the Moabitess said to Naomi…." The image at the top was intended to demonstrate the impoverished situation for Naomi and Ruth upon returning to Bethlehem. Indeed, they had returned because they heard that the Lord had visited his people to give them food (1:6), but they were still considered the "least of these" in the society and needed aid. The table is rather empty to illustrate their poverty and their facial expressions are intended to illustrate their concern of whether (and how) YHWH will provide for them.

<u>Ruth 2:3</u> – וַיִּ֣קֶר מִקְרֶ֔הָ חֶלְקַ֥ת הַשָּׂדֶ֖ה לְבֹ֑עַז... "…and her chance chanced ('she just so happened') upon the portion of the field [belonging] to Boaz." The image at the bottom right of the page is of Boaz even though he is not in the narrative. At various places in the book, we added vignettes of certain characters to draw the reader's attention to that character and the subtle mention of them in the narrative. Here, it is vitally important to the story that Ruth "happened upon" the field of Boaz and so a vignette to Boaz appears.

<u>Ruth 2:4</u> – וְהִנֵּֽה־בֹ֗עַז בָּ֚א מִבֵּ֣ית לֶ֔חֶם וַיֹּ֥אמֶר לַקּוֹצְרִ֖ים יְהוָ֣ה עִמָּכֶ֑ם וַיֹּ֥אמְרוּ ל֖וֹ יְבָרֶכְךָ֥ יְהוָֽה׃ "And behold, Boaz came from Bethlehem and he said to the reapers, 'The Lord [be] with you.' And they said to him, 'May the Lord bless you.'" The facial expressions of the reapers are noteworthy here. There are some who interpret the awkward syntax of the head of the reapers as his social awkwardness when in the presence of Boaz. The facial expressions

of the reapers were intended to convey their sudden reaction when their boss shows up to check in on them.

Ruth 2:9 – ...הֲלֹוא צִוֵּיתִי אֶת־הַנְּעָרִים לְבִלְתִּי נָגְעֵךְ "...have I not commanded the young men to not touch you?" Even though the direct speech depicts Boaz speaking to Ruth, the illustrated scene here is of Boaz commanding his young men not to touch her.

Ruth 2:14 – ...וַתֵּשֶׁב מִצַּד הַקּוֹצְרִים וַיִּצְבָּט־לָהּ קָלִי "and she sat beside the reapers and he held out to her roasted grain." The image at the bottom of the page highlights Ruth's facial expression, one of concern about her situation. While everything seems to be going in the right direction with Boaz and while he seems to be a man of valiant character, she has just been invited to eat dinner with him and his men. Upon this first meeting, surely she had concerns about what may happen to her as a foreign widow among these men. The concern on Ruth's face here will be resolved when she experiences his kindness to provide for her and Naomi.

Ruth 3:4 – This full-page layout depicts the conversation between Naomi and Ruth about their plans at the threshing floor. The smaller images are intended to be vignettes to the fuller images that will come later in the book. At this point in the narrative, Boaz has provided quite lavishly for Naomi and Ruth and so the table that was once bare is now full.

Ruth 3:15b – וַיָּבֹא הָעִיר: "and *he* entered the city." This image depicts Boaz running to Bethlehem, following the manuscript evidence that the verb is a 3ms as opposed to the Syriac and Vulgate that have a 3fs verb ('and she entered the city'). It seems evident that Ruth (3fs) will travel back to the city, and Ruth 3:16 suggests as much (וַתָּבוֹא אֶל־חֲמוֹתָהּ). The last clause in verse 15, however, intends to display Boaz's urgency to address the nearer redeemer in order to redeem Ruth for himself. Naomi affirms Boaz's urgency in 3:18 when she says, "...the man will not stop until the matter is completed today" (כִּי לֹא יִשְׁקֹט הָאִישׁ כִּי־אִם־כִּלָּה הַדָּבָר הַיּוֹם:). Therefore, there is good reason to read 3:15b as Boaz running to the city and this illustration was intended to show that interpretive decision.

<u>Ruth 4:1</u> – וּבֹעַז עָלָה הַשַּׁעַר וַיֵּשֶׁב שָׁם וְהִנֵּה הַגֹּאֵל עֹבֵר אֲשֶׁר דִּבֶּר־בֹּעַז "Now Boaz went up to the gate and he sat down there, and behold the redeemer [was] passing by [about] whom Boaz spoke." The image here portrays Boaz without his robe. The removal of his coat was intended to convey the haste with which he went to the gate of Bethlehem (he was hot from running), and also the providential "speed" at which the nearer redeemer arrived. Boaz has barely had time to take his robe off and sit down. He is still out of breath from the run, "and behold, the redeemer" (וְהִנֵּה הַגֹּאֵל).

<u>Ruth 4:11b</u> – יִתֵּן יְהוָה אֶת־הָאִשָּׁה הַבָּאָה אֶל־בֵּיתֶךָ כְּרָחֵל וּכְלֵאָה אֲשֶׁר בָּנוּ שְׁתֵּיהֶם אֶת־בֵּית יִשְׂרָאֵל "May the Lord make the woman coming into your house like Rachel and like Leah, who together [they] built up the house of Israel." This image is a "vision" back to Jacob and his wives, Rachel and Leah. In this image, Rachel and Leah, along with their respective children are listed as those who "built up the house of Israel." Zilpah and Bilhah are not illustrated here simply because they are not mentioned in Ruth. The other sons of Jacob were born to those two women in order to complete the "house of Israel." In this scene, Judah takes the front stage on Leah's side whereas Joseph takes the front stage on Rachel's side. For Judah, he fathered Perez who will be mentioned in the next verse and at the head of the ending genealogy. For Joseph, he is highlighted as the firstborn son of Jacob's favored wife Rachel. These are the two sons, who as the house of Israel was built up, took prominent roles.

<u>Ruth 4:12</u> – וִיהִי בֵיתְךָ כְּבֵית פֶּרֶץ אֲשֶׁר־יָלְדָה תָמָר לִיהוּדָה "And may your house exist as the house of Perez whom Tamar bore to Judah." This "vision" depicts Judah and Tamar with their twin sons Perez and Zerah (Gen 38:27–30). Perhaps it is a bit too calm of an illustration compared to the sordid situation in which Perez was born to Judah and Tamar, but the moral corruption of the birth does not seem to be what the author of Ruth is highlighting. Rather, the author seems to refer to these stories precisely because they are the ones that illustrate God staying true to his promises even through morally disastrous situations. During the period of the judges in Ruth (1:1), to have a faithful family through whom God would bring about David (4:17, 22) is another example of God building up the house of Israel despite moral bankruptcy in Israel.

<u>Ruth 4:18–22</u> – The image here is the genealogy of Perez with Judah and Tamar at the bottom. The idea to include the names here was a later addition in order to make it clear

that this was a "family tree" of sorts. Therefore, it was difficult to get the names to line up perfectly with where one would expect the names to occur. There is no reason for having Hezron and Ram on the same line with only other names on single lines. The names that are missing from the family tree are assumed to be on the other side of the tree under the writer's hand and this will provide some sense of "balance" to the names on the tree. Overlooking the technical difficulties with this family tree, the theological point is important. Notice that the family tree does not have David at the top. The book of Ruth ends with David, but the theological trajectory of Ruth does not end there. Rather, there is someone else to come after David who will finally and fully rescue Israel from their sinful desperation. Yes, the story of Ruth, Boaz, and Naomi is a picture of a faithful family whom God used to point toward the hope of a redeemer, but even David, as good as he was, was not that redeemer. This genealogy points beyond David, and therefore, the illustration does not end with David even though the book of Ruth does.

Complete Glossary of Words
in the Book of Ruth

א

אָב	father
אָדוֹן	lord
אהב	to love
אָז	then
אֹזֶן	ear
אָח	brother
אֶחָד	one (m)
אחז	to hold, grasp
אַחֵר	other
אַחַר	after
אַחֲרוֹן	last
אֵיךְ	how?
אַיִן	nothing, is not
אֵיפָה	ephah
אֵיפֹה	where?
אִישׁ	man, husband
אֹכֶל	food
אכל	to eat
אֶל	to, toward
אל	no, not
אֱלֹהִים	God
אֱלִימֶלֶךְ	Elimelech
אלְמֹנִי	someone
אֵלֶּה	these
אִם	if
אֵם	mother
אָמָה	handmaid
אמן	to guard, nurse

אָמְנָם	truly
אמץ	to be strong
אמר	to say
אָן	where?
אֲנִי	I, myself
אָנֹכִי	I
אסף	to gather
אֶפְרָתָה	Ephrathah
אֶפְרָתִי	Ephrathite
אֶרֶץ	land, earth
אֲשֶׁר	which
אִשָּׁה	woman, wife
אֵת	(direct object)
אַתְּ	you (f. sing)
אַתָּה	you (m. sing.)
אַתֶּם	you (m. plur.)

ב

בוא	to come
בכה	to weep
בנה	to build
בקשׁ	to seek
ברך	to bless
בְּ	in, at, with
בָּחוּר	young man
בֵּין	between

בֵּית	Beth
בַּיִת	house
בִּלְתִּי	except
בֵּן	son
בֹּעַז	Boaz
בֹּקֶר	morning
בַּת	daughter

ג

גאל	to redeem, avenge
גדל	to grow up, become great
גור	to sojourn, dwell
גלה	to uncover, remove; to go into exile
גער	to rebuke
גְּאֻלָּה	redemption
גִּבּוֹר	mighty
גַּם	also
גֹּרֶן	threshing floor

ד

דבק	to cling
דבר	to speak
דָּבָר	word, speech
דָּוִד	David
דַּל	poor
דֶּרֶךְ	way

ה

הֲ	(interrogative)
הַ	the, Ha
הום	to make a noise
הוּא	he, it
הִיא	she, it
היה	to be
הלך	to walk, go
הֲלֹם	here
הֵם	they (m.)
הִנֵּה	behold
הֵרָיוֹן	pregnancy

ו

וְ	and

ז

זֶה	this (m)
זוּלָה	except, only
זָקֵן	elder, old
זקן	to be old
זרה	to scatter
זֶרַע	seed

ח

חבט	to beat out
חדל	to cease, refrain

חָוָה	to bow, worship
חִטָּה	wheat
חַי	living
חַיִל	strength, wealth, army
חֵיק	bosom
חֶלְקָה	portion
חָמוֹת	mother-in-law
חֹמֶץ	vinegar
חֵן	favor, grace
חֶסֶד	lovingkindness
חסה	to take refuge
חפץ	to delight
חֲצִי	half
חֶצְרוֹן	Hezron
חרד	to tremble, fear

ט

טבל	to dip
טוֹב	pleasant, good
טְרוֹם	before
טֶרֶם	before

י

יְבָמָה	brother's wife
יָד	hand
ידע	to know
יהב	to give, come
יהוה	LORD, GOD
יְהוּדָה	Judah
יוֹם	day
יטב	to be good, pleasing
יכל	to be able
יֶלֶד	child
ילד	to bear, beget
יסף	to add, do again
יצא	to go out
ירא	to fear
ירד	to go down
יֵשׁ	there is
ישׁב	to sit , dwell
יִשַׁי	Jesse
יִשְׂרָאֵל	Israel
יתר	to remain over

כ

כול	to provide, contain
כלה	to be complete, finished
כלם	to be humiliated
כרת	to cut off
כְּ	as, like
כֹּה	thus, here
כִּי	that, because, when
כֹּל	all
כְּלִי	utensil, weapon
כִּלְיוֹן	Chilion
כַּלָּה	daughter-in-law, bride
כָּנָף	wing, edge

ל

לְ	to, Le
לֹא	not, Lo
לֵאָה	Leah
לֵב	heart, Leb
לָהֵן	therefore
לֶחֶם	bread, food, Lehem
לָט	secrecy
לַיְלָה	night
לִין	to lodge, stay over night
לִפַת	to turn, grasp
לקח	to take
לקט	to gather, glean

מ

מְאֹד	very
מדד	to measure
מֹדַעַת	kinsman, relative
מַדּוּעַ	why?
מָה	what?
מוֹאָב	Moab
מוֹאָבִי	Moabite
מוֹדַע	kinsman, relative
מוֹלֶדֶת	native land
מָוֶת	death
מות	to die
מַחְלוֹן	Mahlon
מִטְפַּחַת	cloak
מִי	who?

מכר	to sell
מָלֵא	full
מִן	from
מָנוֹחַ	rest
מְנוּחָה	rest
מֵעֶה	belly
מְעַט	little, few
מצא	to find
מָקוֹם	place
מִקְרֶה	chance
מַר	bitter
מַרְגְּלוֹת	at the feet
מרר	to be bitter
מִשְׁפָּחָה	family
מַשְׂכֹּרֶת	wage

נ

נָא	please, now
נֶגֶד	in front of, opposite
נגד	to tell, declare
נגע	to touch, strike
נגשׁ	to approach
נַחֲלָה	possession
נחם	to comfort, relent
נַחְשׁוֹן	Nahshon
נכר	to recognize, treat as foreign
נָכְרִי	foreign
נַעַל	shoe
נָעֳמִי	Naomi
נַעַר	boy, youth
נַעֲרָה	girl

נפל	to fall	עָנָה	to answer
נֶפֶשׁ	soul	עֶרֶב	evening
נצב	to stand	עֲרֵמָה	heap
נשק	to kiss	עָרְפָּה	Orpah
נשא	to lift, carry, take	עָשִׁיר	rich
נתן	to give, put, set	עשׂה	to do, make
		עֶשֶׂר	ten
		עֲשָׂרָה	ten, -teen
		עֵת	time
		עַתָּה	now

ס

סוך	to anoint
סור	to turn aside

ע

עבר	to pass over, through or by
עגן	to refrain
עֵד	witness
עַד	until, as far as
עוֹבֵד	Obed
עוֹד	again, still, longer
עזב	to forsake, leave
עַיִן	eye, spring, Ain
עִיר	city
עַל	upon, over, above
עלה	to go up
עִם	with
עַם	people
עמד	to stand
עֹמֶר	sheaf
עִמָּד	with
עַמִּינָדָב	Amminadab

פ

פגע	to meet, encounter
פקד	to number, appoint, punish, visit
פרד	to separate
פרשׂ	to spread out
פֹּה	here
פְּלֹנִי	a certain one
פֶּן	lest
פָּנָה	before, face
פֹּעַל	work
פֶּרֶץ	Perez
פַּת	piece

צ

צבט	to hold out
צֶבֶת	bundle
צַד	side

צוה	to command
צמא	to thirst

ק

קבר	to bury
קוֹל	voice
קום	to arise, stand
קָלִי	roasted (grain)
קנה	to buy
קָצֶה	end
קָצִיר	harvest
קצר	to reap
קרא	to call
קרה	to befall. happen
קָרוֹב	near

ר

ראה	to see
רִאשׁוֹן	first, former
רוּת	Ruth
רָחֵל	Rachel
רחץ	to wash, bathe
רֵיקָם	empty
רָם	Ram
רֵעַ	friend, companion, fellow
רָעָב	hunger
רעע	to do evil

שׂ

שׂבַע	abundance
שׂבע	to satisfy, fill
שׂבר	to hope, inspect
שָׂדֶה	field
שֵׂיבָה	gray hair
שׂים	to put, set
שַׂלְמָה	Salmon
שַׂלְמוֹן	Salmon
שׂמְלָה	garment
שְׂעֹרָה	barley

שׁ

שׁאב	to draw
שׁאר	to remain
שֶׁבַע	seven
שׁבת	to cease, rest
שׁבֹּלֶת	ears of grain
שַׁדַּי	Almighty, Shaddai
שׁוב	to return
שׁחת	to destroy, corrupt
שׁית	to put, set
שׁכב	to lie down
שְׁכֵנָה	neighbor
שׁלל	to pull out
שָׁלֵם	whole
שׁלם	to be complete, be sound, pay, make peace
שׁלף	to draw (sword)

שִׁלְשׁוֹם	time past, day before yesterday
שֵׁם	name
שָׁם	there
שׁמע	to hear
שָׁנָה	year
שֵׁנִי	second
שְׁנַיִם	two
שַׁעַר	gate
שִׁפְחָה	maidservant
שׁפט	to judge
שׁקט	to be quiet
שֵׁשׁ	six
שׁתה	to drink

ת

תּוֹלֵדוֹת	generations
תְּחִלָּה	beginning
תַּחַת	under, instead of
תְּמוֹל	previously, yesterday
תְּמוּרָה	exchange
תָּמָר	Tamar
תְּעוּדָה	testimony
תִּקְוָה	hope